TOEFL Idi

Other Kaplan Books for English Learners

TOEFL iBT with CD-ROM, 2008-2009 Edition

Inside the New TOEIC Exam

Inside the TOEFL iBT, Second Edition

TOEFL Vocabulary Quiz Book

Learn English Through Classic Literature Series

The Short Stories and Essays of Mark Twain

American Tales of Horror and the Supernatural

TOEFL® Idioms Quiz Book

428
Toefl

KAPLAN PUBLISHING

New York

TOEFL® is a registered trademark of the Educational Testing Service, which neither sponsors nor endorses this product.

This publication is designed to provide accurate and authoritative information in regard to the subject matter covered. It is sold with the understanding that the publisher is not engaged in rendering legal, accounting, or other professional service. If legal advice or other expert assistance is required, the services of a competent professional should be sought.

© 2008 Kaplan, Inc.

Published by Kaplan Publishing, a division of Kaplan, Inc.
1 Liberty Plaza, 24th Floor
New York, NY 10006

Printed in the United States of America

September 2008
10 9 8 7 6 5 4 3 2 1

ISBN-13: 978-1-4277-9751-3

Kaplan Publishing books are available at special quantity discounts to use for sales promotions, employee premiums, or educational purposes. Please email our Special Sales Department to order or for more information at kaplanpublishing@kaplan.com, or write to Kaplan Publishing, 1 Liberty Plaza, 24th Floor, New York, NY 10006.

HOW TO USE THIS BOOK

The TOEFL (Test of English as a Foreign Language) is a standardized test designed to measure your ability to understand and use English as it is used in a North American university setting. Recent changes to the TOEFL have shifted the focus from how much you know *about* English to how well you comprehend, speak, and write English.

Whether you are taking TOEFL iBT, TOEFL CBT, or TOEFL Pencil-and-Paper, Kaplan's *TOEFL Idioms Quiz Book* is perfectly designed to help you learn over 350 idioms frequently used in English.

An idiom is a word or phrase that has a special meaning apart from its literal translation—it is usually a metaphor. Only people who are good at speaking English will know what an idiom means. Idioms can be difficult to learn, and they require time and patience to master well.

With this book, read the idiom on the front of the page to determine whether you know it; on the reverse side, its definition and a sample sentence are offered to be sure that you understand its correct usage.

Once you have mastered a particular idiom, clip or fold back the corner of the flashcard so that you can skip over it to get to the words you still need to study.

The words are organized according to their part of speech. In some cases, two parts of speech are common, and we have noted these cases with more illustrative examples.

You will also see some notes in square brackets [ ]. This provides additional information about the origins of the idiom that should make it easier to memorize.

In some cases—mainly with verb phrases—some words are interchangeable. In such situations, we have provided two example sentences, one for each version, The most common version appears on the first page.

Study the idioms in any order and start on any page.

Good luck!

to push the envelope
verb

. . . .

to abide by the rules
verb

verb
to do something new and different that goes beyond what was previously thought to be possible; to innovate
*His new website really **pushes the envelope** of what the Internet can be used for.*

• •

verb
to accept and follow (a law, ruling, etc.); to comply with
*Both companies claim the right to sell the product, but they will **abide by** the judge's decision.*

to carry on doing something
verb

· ·

to test the waters
verb

verb

to continue

*The book was so interesting he **carried on** reading it after the end of study hall.*

*They will **carry on** with the dance lessons until they master the tango.*

. . . .

verb

to check the likelihood of success before proceeding

*Before announcing their new initiative, the politicians **tested the waters** by conducting polls on the likely public response.*

to pan out
verb

· ·

to account for a discrepancy
verb

verb

to yield good results; to turn out well

*He has had several job interviews but nothing has **panned out** yet.*

[from *to pan for gold:* to attempt to extract gold from a river]

. . . .

verb

to explain; to be or provide an explanation for

*The police asked him to **account for** the missing money.*

*The full moon **accounts for** the exceptionally high tide today.*

to give away the ending
verb

. . . .

to follow suit
verb

verb
to reveal (information that was supposed to be kept secret)
The party was supposed to be a surprise, but my little sister
gave it away.

· ·

verb
to do the same; to follow the example set by someone else
He decided to skip the tournament and the rest of the team
followed suit.
[a reference to card games in which all players must play a
card of the same suit as the one led by the first player]

to grow out of something
verb

. . . .

to back up data
verb

verb

1. to become too large for (something); to outgrow; 2. to develop on the basis of (something)

*She gives her son's clothes to charity when he **grows out of** them.*

*This book **grew out of** a series of lectures I gave last year.*

· ·

verb

to make an electronic copy (of a computer file, etc.) as security in case the original is damaged or deleted

*The power outage wasn't a problem because we had already **backed up** the files on the computer.*

to know the ropes
verb

· ·

to back someone **into a corner**
verb

verb

to understand how things are done in a particular place

*To succeed in a new job, ask someone who really **knows the ropes** to train you.*

*Hence **to show someone the ropes** means 'to show someone how things are done.'*

[A reference to old-fashioned sailing ships, which had complicated ropes and riggings]

• •

verb

to put (someone or oneself) into a position where there is no way out and no room to maneuver

*His political opponents tried to **back** him **into a corner**, so that any position he took would cause him to lose support.*

*She has **painted** herself **into a corner** by setting the standards so high that no one – including her – can meet them.*

to have second thoughts
verb

· ·

to look after a child
verb

verb
to reconsider
*After I saw the reading list, I **had second thoughts** about taking the class.*

• •

verb
to take care of
*She **looks after** her little brother after school every day.*

KAPLAN

to look forward to an event
verb

. . . .

to look into a suspicious incident
verb

verb

to anticipate (something) with pleasure

*I'm **looking forward to** the concert next week.*

. . . .

verb

to investigate; to seek information about

*We are **looking into** buying a camper for our summer trip.*

to keep one's options open
verb

· ·

to bring the facts **home** to her
verb

verb

to avoid doing anything that might rule out a future course of action

*He will probably matriculate to State University, but he's **keeping his options open** until he has gotten a response from all of the schools he applied to.*

- -

verb

to make (the reality of something) clear

*This book finally **brought** the complexity of the issue **home** to me.*

to bring new information **to light**
verb

• •

to see the light
verb

verb
to reveal; to uncover
*Their study **brought to light** some long-forgotten manuscripts.*

. . . .

verb
to finally realize something after serious consideration
*I thought he would never agree with me, but eventually he **saw the light**.*

to look up
verb

. . . .

to look something **up**
verb

verb
to show signs of improvement
*She had more tests done and the doctors say her health is **looking up**.*

. . . .

verb
to seek information about (something) in a reference work
*I **looked up** the words I didn't know in a dictionary.*

to look up to someone
verb

· ·

to give someone **free rein**
verb

verb

to have respect and admiration for (someone)

*He had always **looked up to** his uncle, who was a teacher.*

. . . .

verb

to put few restrictions on the behavior of (someone)

*The new teacher **gives** the students **free rein** to study whatever they want.*

See to rein someone in.

[A rein is the strap used to control a horse while riding.]

to rein someone **in**
verb

· ·

to give her story **the benefit of the doubt**
verb

verb

to control (someone's) behavior closely

*Whenever he began to stray from the task our supervisor **reined** him **in**.*

See to give someone free rein.

· ·

verb

to assume that (a person or statement) is truthful until proven otherwise

*His alibi is suspicious, but let's **give** him **the benefit of the doubt** until we know more.*

to hold one's own
verb

· ·

to hold one's tongue
verb

verb

to perform reasonably well in a challenging situation

*The other runners in the race are much more experienced, but **he is holding his own** and will probably finish right in the middle.*

* *

verb

to stay silent; to refrain from speaking

*She was upset and wanted to say something, but she **held her tongue**.*

to bring something to **mind**
verb

· ·

to set the record straight
verb

verb
to be reminiscent of (something); to remind
*This dish **brings to mind** a meal I once had in Paris.*

. . . .

verb
to correct a false story; to provide accurate information
*The media initially reported that the escaped animal was a
tiger, but zoo officials **set the record straight**, announcing that
it was a harmless kangaroo.*

to use up a resource
verb

. . . .

to size up the competition
verb

verb

to consume (something) completely

*I couldn't brush my teeth this morning because my brother had **used up** the toothpaste.*

· ·

verb

to evaluate or assess

*The dogs growled and walked in a circle, **sizing** each other **up**.*

to have one's hands tied
verb

· ·

to lower the bar
verb

verb

to be restricted; to be prevented from doing something

*I wish I could give you more information, but **my hands are tied**.*

*The government was unable to respond quickly because **its hands were tied** by regulations.*

. . . .

verb

to reduce standards so that it is easier to succeed

*When no one qualified under the original criteria, the admissions committee **lowered the bar**.*

to flare up
verb

· ·

to ask after someone
verb

verb
to erupt or break out; to recur
My doctor had said the rash on my knee was cured, but it **flared up** *again.*

· ·

verb
to inquire about the well-being of (someone)
He heard your mother was in the hospital and called to **ask after** *her.*

to hold sway
verb

· ·

to go through with it
verb

verb
to dominate; to have great influence
*The Dutch **held sway** in New York until 1664, when the English took control.*

. . . .

verb
to perform (an action) as planned; to carry out
*We **went through with** our plan to have a picnic in spite of the rain.*

to end up
verb

· ·

to lay claim to property
verb

verb

to come eventually to a particular situation or place

*It **ended up** costing much more than we expected.*

*After walking for hours, they **ended up** in the same place where they started.*

. . . .

verb

to assert that one has the right to (something); to claim ownership of

*My sister always **laid claim** to the top bunk bed, so I was stuck on the bottom.*

to cross one's mind
verb

. . . .

to hold on to shares in the company
verb

verb
to occur to one
*I'm so accustomed to flying that the possibility of driving home
never **crossed my mind**.*

· ·

verb
to keep or retain
*He considered selling his motorcycle, but he decided to **hold on
to** it.*

to hold out
verb

• •

to leave no stone unturned
verb

verb
to resist or endure in a challenging situation
*Her doctor advised her to give up meat, and she **held out** for six months before giving in to temptation.*

• •

verb
to look everywhere; to attempt everything
*We **left no stone unturned** in our search for the city's best hot dog.*

to cross paths
verb

· ·

to run into someone
verb

verb
to meet by chance
*They **crossed paths** in Italy when they both happened to be vacationing there.*
*He **crossed paths** with my sister in college.*

• •

verb
to meet (someone) by chance
*I hadn't seen him in months, but I **ran into** him at the super-market last week.*

to have one's work cut out for
verb

· ·

to get one's act together
verb

verb
to have a lot of work to do in order to accomplish something
*If she wants to finish this drawing before the art fair **she has her work cut out for her**.*

. . . .

verb
to prepare oneself to accomplish something; to get organized
*We need to **get our act together** if we're going to finish this by Friday.*

to drop by
verb

. . . .

to drop in on someone
verb

verb
to make a short, usually unannounced, visit
*He **dropped by** for a few minutes last night.*

· ·

verb
to make a short, usually unannounced, visit to (a person)
*On the way home we **dropped in on** my grandmother to see how she was doing.*

to have one's hands full
verb

. . . .

to go wrong
verb

verb
to be very busy; to have a lot to do
*She has **had her hands full** lately, so she probably won't be able to help you.*

∙ ∙

verb
to cause a failure; to go amiss
*The experiment failed, but scientists still aren't sure what **went wrong**.*

to err on the side of caution
verb

. . . .

to rest on one's laurels
verb

verb

to emphasize (a particular aspect of an issue) so that if a mistake is made it will enhance that aspect

*No one knows what level of pollutants is safe for fish, so it seems best to **err on the side of** conservation by stopping all pollution in the river.*

. . . .

verb

to be satisfied with one's past accomplishments rather than attempting anything new

*Since his highly praised first novel came out he has been **resting on his laurels** and hasn't written anything new.*

[a reference to the ancient Greek tradition of crowning a person with a wreath of laurels, or bay leaves, to honor a great accomplishment]

to take one's time
verb

• •

to tighten one's belt
verb

verb

to proceed slowly; to avoid rushing

*I'm **taking my time** on this paper, since it isn't due until the end of the semester.*

. . . .

verb

to take extreme measures in order to economize; to cut back

*Our funding has been cut, so we are going to have **to tighten our belts** and reduce the budget.*

[a reference to losing weight from eating less, which might cause someone to need a smaller belt]

to touch on a subject
verb

• •

to see eye to eye
verb

verb
to address (a topic) briefly
*The course will mainly cover the works of Jean-Jacques Rousseau, but it will also **touch on** some of his contemporaries, such as Voltaire and Diderot.*

• •

verb
to have similar opinions; to understand each other
*They have almost nothing in common, but when it comes to baseball they **see eye to eye**.*

to have a say
verb

· ·

to cherry-pick
verb

verb

to have a degree of influence or power

*It is important for children to **have a say** in decisions about their activities.*

*In a democracy, citizens **have a voice** in their government.*

• •

verb

to take only the most desirable items available from among a selection

*She sells the most cars because she **cherry-picks** the most promising customers, leaving the rest of us with the reluctant ones.*

to do someone **good**
verb

. . . .

to narrow down a list
verb

verb

to have a beneficial effect on (someone)

*He has seemed very stressed out lately; a vacation will **do him good**.*

. . . .

verb

to reduce the number of options in (a selection)

*They started with a pool of twenty applicants, but they **narrowed** it **down** to three finalists.*

to draw a blank
verb

• •

to do one's best
verb

verb
to be unable to remember or respond
*I studied thoroughly for the test, but when I saw the first question I just **drew a blank**.*

. . . .

verb
to try as hard as possible
*He didn't get a perfect score, but he **did his best**, and that is what really matters.*

to throw down the gauntlet
verb

. . . .

to throw in the towel
verb

verb
to issue a challenge
*The American colonists **threw down the gauntlet** to England in 1776 with the Declaration of Independence.*
[A gauntlet is a type of armored glove, which would traditionally be thrown down by a medieval knight in a challenge to an opponent. To accept the challenge, the opponent would pick up the glove; hence to take up the gauntlet means 'to accept a challenge.']

• •

verb
to accept defeat; to surrender
*After struggling for many years with our business, we finally **threw in the towel** after realizing we needed to make major renovations.*

to throw someone **to the wolves**
verb

· ·

to fill someone **in**
verb

verb

to leave (someone) to face criticism or challenges alone; to abandon (someone)

*He claimed not to know anything about the scandal and **threw his assistant to the wolves**.*

. . . .

verb

to inform (someone) fully; to give (someone) the details

*Lisa missed the meeting where that was discussed, so someone will have to **fill** her **in**.*

to fill in for someone
verb

· ·

to take someone's **place**
verb

verb
to replace or substitute for
*I usually work on Mondays and Fridays, but I'm **filling in for** Mark today.*

· ·

verb
to replace or substitute for (someone)
*The star of the play got sick, so the understudy **took** her **place**.*

to come to grips with a challenging concept
verb

. . . .

to stay out of a dispute
verb

verb

to become capable of dealing with or understanding

Many companies still haven't **come to grips with** *the new regulations.*

It took us a long time to **get to grips with** *this computer program.*

● ●

verb

to avoid getting involved in

The United States **stayed out** *of the First World War until April of 1917.*

to wear thin
verb

· ·

to speak out on a controversial issue
verb

verb

to become less effective due to overuse
*You claim to have forgotten your homework at least once a week, so that excuse is **wearing thin**.*

• •

verb

to express one's opinions openly
*It was nice to hear a politician **speak out** about the problems facing farmers today.*

to think up a new game
verb

· ·

to take advantage of someone or something
verb

verb

to invent; to make up

*Our math teacher is always **thinking up** new ways to make sure we do our homework.*

. . . .

verb

1. to exploit (someone); 2. to utilize or avail oneself of (something)

*They were only taking **advantage of him**, and had no interest in really being his friends.*

*She is trying **to take advantage of** the many cultural experiences the city has to offer.*

to carry out orders
verb

· ·

to meet someone **halfway**
verb

verb
to obey; to put into action
*He **carried out** your instructions perfectly; everything is the way you wanted it.*

· ·

verb
to compromise with (someone)
*We made several good offers, but he stubbornly stuck to his original price and refused to **meet us halfway**.*

to meet one's match
verb

. . . .

to keep a low profile
verb

verb
to find one's equal
*He is a great chess player, but in you he finally **met his match**.*

· ·

verb
to avoid getting attention or publicity
*Like many celebrities, she started **keeping a low profile** after she had children.*

to get a message **across**
verb

. . . .

to get away with a crime
verb

verb

to express

*The president's latest speech really **got across** his concern about the need for more educational funding.*

• •

verb

to manage to escape the consequences of (an action)

*I can't believe he **got away with** cheating on that quiz.*

to think on one's feet
verb

• •

to wash one's hands of the whole affair
verb

verb
to react quickly and effectively without prior preparation
*She had to **think on her feet** when she was unexpectedly asked to lead the discussion.*

· ·

verb
to claim to no longer be responsible for or involved with (something); to dissociate oneself from
*He has **washed his hands of** the group since it participated in a controversial protest last year.*

to settle for a lower price
verb

. . . .

to cast doubt on something
verb

verb

to accept less than desired or expected
*He had dreamed of becoming president, but he **settled for** being mayor of a small town.*

• •

verb

to make (something) appear doubtful or dubious
*The photos from the party **cast doubt on** his version of events.*

to make a point of doing something
verb

• •

to make do
verb

verb
to make a deliberate effort to do something
*I **make a point** of calling my grandmother once a week.*

. . . .

verb
to manage without something important; to get by
*During the Second World War cooks often **made do** without rationed ingredients like chocolate and sugar.*

to make sure
verb

· ·

to make sense
verb

verb
to be certain; to confirm
*Before leaving the house he **made sure** he had his keys.*

• •

verb
to be reasonable or logical
*Her theory **makes sense**.*

to keep an eye on something
verb

· ·

to get over a setback
verb

verb
to watch; to monitor
*Could you please **keep an eye on** the cake in the oven and make sure it doesn't burn?*

· ·

verb
to recover from; to bounce back from
*She is finally **getting over** her cold.*
*The team needs to **get over** today's loss and start preparing for the next game.*

to take someone's **word for it**
verb

· ·

to take a break
verb

verb
to believe someone without additional evidence
*He says that he didn't take the money, and I'm **taking** his **word for it**.*

. . . .

verb
to take a rest; to stop an activity temporarily
*She painted for hours at a time without **taking a break**.*

to draw the line
verb

· ·

to think better of a decision
verb

verb

to set a limit about how far one is willing to go

*She is an adventurous eater, but she **draws the line** at insects.*

*I'll help you out one more time, but that is where **I draw the line**.*

. . . .

verb

to decide against (doing something) after thinking about it more; to reconsider

*He had planned to take part in the prank, but he **thought better of it** and stayed home.*

to think something **over**
verb

• •

to think twice
verb

verb
to consider (something) carefully
*I probably won't accept the job offer, but I am still **thinking it over**.*

. . . .

verb
to consider carefully before making a decision
*If I were you, I would **think twice** about buying a used car over the Internet.*
*When he was invited to give a speech at his old high school, he didn't **think twice** before agreeing.*

to get rid of something
verb

· ·

to get the best of someone
verb

verb
to discard or eliminate
*We **got rid of** all the food in the refrigerator that was past its due date.*

• •

verb
to defeat or outwit
*He tried to stay awake for the fireworks at midnight, but his fatigue **got the best of** him and he fell asleep before 11:00.*

to get to the bottom of a mystery
verb

· ·

to get underway
verb

verb
to uncover the truth about
*We reported the strange sounds coming from the house next door and the police promised **to get to the bottom of** it.*

● ●

verb
to begin; to start
*The annual Autumn Festival **gets underway** next week.*

to mince words
verb

● ●

to jump on the bandwagon
verb

verb

to avoid directly saying something which might upset or offend; to euphemize

*Tell me what you really thought of my performance and don't **mince words**.*

· ·

verb

to take up an activity or idea that is suddenly very popular

*The price of the stock rose quickly as investors **jumped on the bandwagon** and bought shares.*

*She has listened to their music for years, but now everyone is **getting on the bandwagon**.*

to make good on a promise
verb

. . . .

to make off with the money
verb

verb
to follow through on
*The company **made good on** its pledge to donate new computers to the school.*

• •

verb
to take or steal (something); to abscond with
*He was caught after the party trying to **make off with** two silver vases.*

to stand for
verb

· ·

to stand up for someone
verb

verb
1. to support or advocate (a belief or principle); 2. to be an abbreviation of
*The memorial should express the ideals he **stood for** all his life: freedom and equality.*
*FBI **stands for** Federal Bureau of Investigation.*

· ·

verb
to defend; to advocate for
*She always **stood up for** her little brother when other children teased him.*

to stand out
verb

• •

to wind down
verb

verb
to be conspicuous; to attract attention
*The white flowers **stand out** against the dark background of the painting.*

• •

verb
1. to slow down, to draw to a close; 2. to relax (said of a person)
*The wedding season hits its peak in June and starts to **wind down** in September.*
*After three days of tough hiking, we spent a day **winding down** at the beach.*

to wind up somewhere
verb

• •

to keep at a task
verb

verb

to find oneself in a place or situation; to arrive or end up

*I was as surprised as anyone when **I wound up** in the television industry.*

• •

verb

to continue to do; to persist or persevere with

*She had trouble at first, but she **kept at** it and is now one of the best gymnasts in the state.*

to keep information **from** someone
verb

. . . .

to keep from doing something
verb

verb

to hide (something) from someone; to keep (something)
secret from someone

*Romeo and Juliet **kept** their marriage **from** their families.*

· ·

verb

to stop oneself from doing something; to refrain from or
avoid

*When she saw his new haircut she could hardly **keep from**
laughing.*

to keep up with someone or something
verb

. . . .

to lend a hand
verb

verb

1. to travel at the same speed as; to stay abreast of; 2. to stay informed about

*He couldn't **keep up with** the other cyclists on the hilly part of the course.*

*I try to **keep up with** the latest advances in computer science.*

• •

verb

to help

*Local charities **lent a hand** to the effort to rebuild after the earthquake.*

*Could you please **give me a hand** with this heavy box?*

to jump to conclusions
verb

• •

to sit around
verb

verb

to form an opinion about something quickly without examining all of the facts

*A good doctor looks at all of a patient's symptoms carefully before making a diagnosis rather than just **jumping to conclusions**.*

· ·

verb

to lounge or be idle; to hang around

*He used to exercise a lot, but now he just **sits around** playing video games.*

to sit through a long ceremony
verb

• •

to sit tight
verb

verb

to stay to the end of (an event or performance)

*I wanted to leave the play at intermission but my parents made me **sit through** all three hours of it.*

· ·

verb

to wait patiently

*Could you just **sit tight** for a little bit longer? I'm almost ready to leave.*

to get on with an activity
verb

· ·

to take a piece of information **into account**
verb

verb

to continue

*We need to stop wasting time and **get on with** studying for the exam.*

• •

verb

to consider; to give attention to

*The theory was flawed because it didn't **take into account** the importance of environmental factors.*

to show up
verb

· ·

to show someone **up**
verb

verb
to arrive
*She didn't **show up** at work until after 11:00 am.*

• •

verb
to embarrass or outperform (someone)
*He **showed up** the team captain by making the most goals in last night's game.*

to split hairs
verb

• •

to go without saying
verb

verb
to make small, unimportant distinctions
*They still haven't agreed on the final wording of the contract, but they are just **splitting hairs** now; all of the important issues have been decided.*

• •

verb
to be obvious or self-evident
*It **goes without saying** that you should wear respectful clothes to a job interview.*

to take something **in stride**
verb

• •

to wipe something **out**
verb

verb

to deal with (something difficult) in a calm way, so that it does not cause disruptions

*The players **took** the insults of the opposing team **in stride** and focused on winning the game.*

• •

verb

to destroy (something) completely

*Three years of drought **wiped out** the region's agriculture.*

to save one's breath
verb

. . . .

to save face
verb

verb

to refrain from saying something that is useless or unnecessary

*She won't stop smoking no matter what you say; **save your breath**.*

• •

verb

to preserve one's dignity or honor; to avoid embarrassment

*He **saved face** by resigning from his job before he could be fired.*

to fill out a form
verb

· ·

to bide one's time
verb

verb
to complete (a form)
*He has **filled out** all of his college applications.*

· ·

verb
to wait patiently
*She's living with her parents for a while, **biding her time** until she finds the right apartment.*

to keep her **on** her **toes**
verb

· ·

to keep track of
verb

verb
to force (someone) to stay alert
*Our teacher **keeps us on our toes** by asking questions throughout his lectures.*

• •

verb
to keep a record of; to stay informed about
*She **kept track of** her expenses so that she could be reimbursed.*

to slip someone's **mind**
verb

· ·

to pave the way
verb

verb

to be forgotten by someone
*I was supposed to buy milk on the way home but it completely **slipped my mind**.*

. . . .

verb

to make future accomplishments possible; to prepare the way
*The achievements of pioneering female scientists like Marie Curie **paved the way** for later generations of women in science.*
[*Way* is an old-fashioned word for road; *paving* a road makes it easier and faster to travel on.]

to take it easy
verb

• •

That name is starting **to ring a bell.**
verb

verb
to relax; to be idle
*Last summer I worked 40 hours a week, but this year I am **taking it easy**.*

• •

verb
to bring back a memory; to sound familiar
*I don't recognize her face, but her voice **rings a bell**.*

to put the rumors **to rest**
verb

· ·

to pin down the details
verb

verb
to put a stop to; to end; to quell
*If you are afraid of flying, the new technology in these planes should **put** your fears **to rest**.*

· ·

verb
to define firmly; to figure out
*The wedding is supposed to be this summer but they haven't **pinned down** the date yet.*

to field questions
verb

. . . .

to count as
verb

verb

to answer questions from a group of people

*After his speech, he **fielded questions** from the audience.*

• •

verb

to be considered; to qualify as

*Astronomy 101 **counts as** a science course for the school's distri-bution requirement.*

to count on
verb

• •

to keep a threat **at bay**
verb

verb

to rely on; to depend on

*We need to be home early because Mom is **counting on** us to help her with dinner.*

. . . .

verb

to make (something) stay away; to ward off

*I've been **keeping** the flu **at bay** by resting and drinking lots of orange juice.*

*The moat around the castle was designed to **hold** invaders at **bay**.*

to figure out
verb

• •

to cut back on long-distance phone calls
verb

verb
to determine or conclude
*The mechanic **figured out** that the problems were being caused by a leak in my car's fuel line.*

. . . .

verb
to use or do less of (something)
*His doctor told him that he should **cut back on** sugar.*

to cut off
verb

• •

to cut to the chase
verb

verb
1. to interrupt; 2. to stop or discontinue
*She rudely **cut** him **off** in the middle of his story.*
*The storm **cut off** the city's supply of electricity.*

. . . .

verb
to get directly to the point
*He started describing all of the different features, but we were in a hurry so we asked him to **cut to the chase**.*

to come around
verb

. . . .

to come down to
verb

verb
to agree to something eventually
*My father didn't like the idea of me going to college so far away from home, but I'm sure he'll **come around**.*

· ·

verb
to have as an essential point; to be dependent upon
*There are all sorts of fad diets around, but healthy weight loss **comes down to** two factors: eating well and exercising regularly.*

to come along
verb

· ·

to bear fruit
verb

verb
1. to accompany; 2. to progress
He invited a friend to **come along.**
There were a lot of construction problems at first, but the new house is finally **coming along.**

· ·

verb
to produce results; to be successful
After twenty years of research, our effort to cure the disease is finally **bearing fruit.**

to take its toll
verb

· ·

to put off a meeting
verb

verb
to have a negative effect
*The drought **took its toll** on the crops, and the harvest was much smaller than usual.*
*She looks exhausted. All of those late nights of studying are finally **taking their toll**.*

· ·

verb
to postpone
*Our teacher **put** the test **off** until next week.*

to pass up an opportunity
verb

• •

to put one's finger on a piece of information
verb

verb
to decline; to fail to take advantage of
*She **passed up** a scholarship at a prestigious university because the school didn't have a good soccer team.*

. . . .

verb
to identify; to pinpoint
*There must be something missing but I can't **put my finger on** what it is.*

to turn a blind eye to a problem
verb

• •

to take note of the changes
verb

verb
to ignore; to overlook
*The superintendent accused local schools of **turning a blind eye** to plagiarism and cheating.*

. . . .

verb
to notice; to observe
*He didn't immediately **take note of** her new haircut.*

to fall into place
verb

· ·

to fall out with someone
verb

verb

to turn out as hoped for

*We were afraid that we would never finish planning our wedding, but everything seems to be **falling into place**.*

· ·

verb

to have a serious disagreement

*They **fell out with** each other years ago over who would run the family business.*

*Also as a noun: to have a **falling-out** with someone.*

to fall short
verb

• •

to muddle through
verb

verb
to fail to meet expectations
*Our profits for last year **fell short**.*

. . . .

verb
to find a way in spite of difficulty or disorganization; to manage
*I didn't know anything about how to direct a play, but I **muddled through**.*

to bring someone **up to date**
verb

. . . .

to put a project **on hold**
verb

verb
to give (someone) the latest information
Since you have been absent, talk to me after class and I will **bring** *you* **up to date.**

· ·

verb
to stop (something) temporarily; to suspend
We are **putting** *the renovation* **on hold** *until next summer.*

to rule out a possibility
verb

. . . .

to play down an achievement
verb

verb

to exclude (something) as a possible option or explanation

*We haven't decided where to spend our honeymoon yet, but we have **ruled out** going on a cruise.*

*The doctor told her that tests had **ruled out** cancer as the cause of her symptoms.*

• •

verb

to minimize the importance of

*The other students were impressed by her famous father, but she always **played down** her glamorous background.*

The opposite is *to play up* 'to exaggerate'

to play it safe
verb

· ·

to play with fire
verb

verb
to avoid taking risks
*They **played it safe** and allowed two hours for the drive to the airport.*

. . . .

verb
to do something dangerous or risky
*We warned the diplomat that he was **playing with fire** by getting involved in local politics.*

to keep something **in mind**
verb

• •

to bargain for
verb

verb

to remember and account for (something)

*While writing your essay, **keep in mind** that you will get a higher grade if it has a clear argument.*

· ·

verb

to expect or be prepared for

*The vacationers got more rain than they had **bargained for** when monsoon season hit a few weeks early.*

to deal with a problem
verb

• •

to take over the company
verb

verb
to handle or control
*They are finding new ways of **dealing with** the rising cost of college tuition.*

. . . .

verb
to take control of
*He is difficult to work because he usually tries to **take over** the most interesting projects.*

to run out of provisions
verb

. . . .

to take on someone or something
verb

verb
to use up (a supply of something)
*I couldn't make cookies because I **ran out** of sugar.*

. . . .

verb
1. to hire (an employee); 2. to confront; to fight against
*They decided to **take** him **on** as a research assistant.*
*The environmental group is **taking on** a big corporation it accuses of polluting the lake.*

to beat around the bush
verb

• •

to put down roots
verb

verb
to avoid talking directly about something
*The community meeting was frustrating, because the mayor
kept **beating around the bush** instead of addressing the important issues facing our community.*

. . . .

verb
to settle down; to establish a permanent residence
*After years of traveling, he is finally **putting down roots** by
buying a house in his hometown.*

to put up with something unpleasant
verb

· ·

to take part
verb

verb
to endure or tolerate
*Rather than disciplining students who are late for class, she **puts up with** their behavior.*

. . . .

verb
to participate
*Fifty nations **took part** in the conference at which the Charter of the United Nations was drafted in 1945.*

to take sides
verb

• •

to talk someone **into doing** something
verb

verb

to align oneself with one of the sides in a dispute

*Parents should avoid **taking sides** when their children argue.*

. . . .

verb

to convince (someone) to do something

*He didn't want to join the team, but they **talked** him **into** it.*

to put the cart before the horse
verb

· ·

to make up one's mind
verb

verb
to do things in the wrong order
Critics say that buying furniture for the new library before the architect has been chosen is **putting the cart before the horse**.

• •

verb
to decide; to make a decision
He got into three different colleges, so now he is trying to **make up his mind** *about which one to attend.*

to pay the price for a crime
verb

. . . .

to take a stab at doing something
verb

verb
to bear the consequences of a mistake or misdeed
*The school principal made the whole class **pay the price** for graffiti made by one student.*

. . . .

verb
to try; to make an attempt
*I've never baked a pie before, but I'm **taking a stab at** it this weekend.*
*They asked him to **make a stab at** creating a web page.*

to part with a possession
verb

· ·

to take something **with a grain of salt**
verb

verb
to give (something) up
*Even when he went to college, he refused **to part with** his teddy bear.*

. . . .

verb
to be skeptical about (something)
*Since he has strong views on this subject, so I **took** his report **with a grain of salt**.*

to have egg on one's face
verb

· ·

to wear many hats
verb

verb
to be embarrassed
*When the newspaper published the article about his company's financial problems, the executive **had egg on his face**.*

. . . .

verb
to fill many roles
*As a mother, teacher, volunteer, and musician, she **wears many hats** in her everyday life.*

worth one's salt
adjective

· ·

off guard
adjective

adjective
competent at one's profession
*Any coach **worth his salt** would have taught you how to stretch your muscles after practice.*

. . . .

adjective
unprepared
*She did well for most of the interview, but she was caught **off guard** by the last question.*

on an even keel
adjective

. . . .

above board
adjective

adjective
steady and balanced; moving calmly forward
*The local economy went through some difficult times when the factory closed, but it has been **on an even keel** for many years.*
Also **even-keeled:** *She has an **even-keeled** personality.*
[A *keel* is a structure on the bottom of a boat that keeps it stable.]

. . . .

adjective
conducted lawfully and openly; legitimate; honest
*The deal sounded suspicious, but my lawyer assured me that it was completely **above board**.*
See *under the table*.

blue collar
adjective

. . . .

white collar
adjective

adjective
involving or denoting physical labor
*During the summer he does **blue collar** jobs like construction work and house painting.*
See *white collar.*

· ·

adjective
denoting administrative or clerical work that does not involve physical labor
*The Internet boom has created a lot of office jobs for **white-collar** workers.*
See *blue collar.*

run of the mill
adjective

. . . .

on the tip of one's tongue
adjective

adjective
unexceptional; ordinary
*Despite all of the attention he has gotten in the press, I think he is really just a **run-of-the-mill** portrait painter.*

. . . .

adjective
on the verge of being recalled
*I can't quite remember his name, but it's **on the tip of my tongue**.*

beside the point
adjective

• •

to the point
adjective

adjective
irrelevant; unimportant
*The real issue in the renovation is that we need more space; the color of the carpet is **beside the point**.*
See *to the point*.

. . . .

adjective
directly related to the topic at hand; relevant
*The testimony of the star witness in the case was concise and **to the point**.*
See *beside the point*

at a loss for words
adjective

. . . .

neither here nor there
adjective

adjective
unable to think of anything to say; speechless
*When they told her father they were getting married, he was **at a loss for words**.*

. . . .

adjective
unimportant or irrelevant
*We accept anyone who can play chess; your age is **neither here nor there**.*

down to earth
adjective

. . . .

down and out
adjective

adjective

reasonable and practical; realistic

*She seems remarkably **down to earth** for the daughter of a wealthy celebrity.*

- -

adjective

very poor; destitute

*A decade ago he was a **down-and-out** alcoholic, but today he owns his own business and has been sober for 8 years.*

in check
adjective

. . . .

beside oneself
adjective

adjective
under control
Now that our rent is higher, we will have to keep our spending ***in check***.

• •

adjective
extremely agitated or upset; distraught
He came home three hours late and his mother was ***beside*** ***herself*** *with worry.*

full-fledged
adjective

· ·

a **no-win** predicament
adjective

adjective
complete; mature; fully developed
*Her hobby of baking cookies has become a **full-fledged** business, with stores all over the city.*

· ·

adjective
having no possibility of a positive outcome
*It was a **no-win** situation: we either had to pay the fine or pay a lawyer to fight it.*
See win-win.

a **win-win** situation
adjective

• •

in charge of
adjective

adjective
denoting a situation in which both parties benefit
*He will get professional experience and you will get a web page at a discount: it's a **win-win** arrangement.*
Also (informally) as a noun: *it was a **win-win**.*

· ·

adjective
responsible for; in control of
*You will be **in charge of** refreshments for our next meeting.*

on the right track
adjective

· ·

on the wrong track
adjective

adjective
following a course that is likely to be successful
*I don't know the answer yet but I think I am **on the right track**.*
See *on the wrong track*.

· ·

adjective
following a course that is likely to fail
*He hasn't been making progress with his research and seems to be **on the wrong track**.*
See *on the right track*.

on the fence
adjective

• •

on the horizon
adjective

adjective
undecided; unable to make up one's mind
He is still on the fence about which candidate to vote for.

. . . .

adjective
coming up in the future
We aren't very busy at the moment, but we have some major projects on the horizon.

red-handed
adjective

· ·

'FYI' is **short for** 'for your information'.
adjective

adjective
in the act of committing a crime
*They caught the thief **red-handed**, with the stolen jewelry in his pockets.*

. . . .

adjective
used as an abbreviation or shortened form of
*Did you know that the word 'pram' is **short for** 'perambulator'?*

wrapped up in something
adjective

. . . .

up in the air
adjective

adjective
preoccupied with; completely absorbed in
*He was so **wrapped up in** the baseball game on television that he didn't hear me walk in.*

. . . .

adjective
unresolved; not yet settled
*We are going to go on vacation this summer, but we haven't decided where yet; our plans are still **up in the air**.*

in short supply
adjective

· ·

low-key
adjective

adjective
scarce; insufficiently available; running out
*We have plenty of food left, but water is **in short supply**.*

. . . .

adjective
relaxed; laid-back; restrained
*We are having a party but it won't be anything big, just a **low-key** gathering of friends.*

feeling **up to** it
adjective

· ·

in the pipeline
adjective

adjective
ready for or able to do something
*It is a very steep mountain; are you sure you're **up to** the hike?*

• •

adjective
on the way; being developed
*She published two books last year and she already has another one **in the pipeline**.*

on the same page
adjective

. . . .

in touch with someone
adjective

adjective
in complete agreement
*They had some arguments about the renovation in the beginning, but now they are **on the same page**.*

. . . .

adjective
in contact with; in communication with
*We used to be close friends, but I haven't been **in touch with** him for several years now.*
*I really hope that I will keep **in touch with** my college roommates after we graduate.*

at a premium
adjective

. . . .

in the wings
adjective

adjective
particularly valuable; especially in demand
*In today's job market, computer skills are **at a premium**.*

· ·

adjective
ready to act or be used at any time
*Newspaper columnists often keep one idea **in the wings** in case of writer's block.*
*There were many people waiting **in the wings** to take over when she retired.*
[a reference to the *wings* of a theater, where actors wait to go on stage]

in the works
adjective

• •

in line with regulations
adjective

adjective
being planned or produced; in process
*A sequel to that movie is **in the works**.*

• •

adjective
in accordance with; consistent with
*The themes of her most recent novel are **in line** with her previous work.*

at the mercy of a few powerful people
adjective

• •

on top of a task
adjective

adjective
completely under the control of; powerless against; totally
dependent upon
*Medieval peasants were often **at the mercy of** their local over-*
lord.
*The small ship was **at the mercy of** the storm.*

. . . .

adjective
doing everything necessary to accomplish (something); in
control of
I offered her help with the decorations for the dance, but she
*said she was **on top of it**.*

time-honored
adjective

. . . .

on the table
adjective

adjective
traditional; long-standing
*Serving turkey with cranberry sauce at Thanksgiving is a **time-honored** custom in the United States.*

· ·

adjective
up for discussion; possible as an option
*We haven't made a final decision yet, so all of the proposals are still **on the table**.*

a man of few words
adjective

. . . .

out of the question
adjective

adjective

not talkative; reticent

*My grandmother is a woman **of few words**, but when she says something it is usually very insightful.*

. . . .

adjective

impossible; inconceivable; not worth considering

*Because of the recent snowstorm, driving over the mountain was **out of the question**.*

worse for wear
adjective

· ·

thin-skinned
adjective

adjective
showing signs of age or use
This sofa was beautiful when it was new, but it is getting a bit **worse for wear**.

· ·

adjective
extremely sensitive; easily upset
When students are too **thin-skinned**, *it can be difficult to give them feedback on their work.*
The opposite is *thick-skinned*.

light years ahead
adjective

. . . .

out of hand
adjective

adjective
far ahead; far more advanced
*Their science laboratories are **light years ahead** of the facilities at our university.*

· ·

adjective
unmanageable; out of control
*The absenteeism in this class is getting **out of hand**.*

a grass-roots effort
adjective

• •

fine tuning
adjective

adjective
based on the efforts of ordinary people
*Our new city councilwoman didn't get a lot of support from powerful politicians, but she had a strong **grass-roots** campaign.*
Also as a noun: *support from the **grass roots**.*

• •

noun
minor adjustments needed to perfect something
*The car is running now, but we have to do some **fine tuning** to make it ready to drive on the road.*
Also as a verb: *We need to **fine-tune** our performance.*

easy as pie
adjective

. . . .

one in a million
adjective

adjective
very simple
*Since he had studied so hard, he thought the exam was **easy as pie**.*

• •

adjective
unique; unusual
*The company knew they'd found **one in a million** when they hired her for the job.*

wet behind one's ears
adjective

. . . .

green
adjective

adjective
new; untested
*He doesn't know yet how his company's e-mail system works, because he's only been here one day and is still **wet behind the ears**.*

. . . .

adjective
inexperienced; new
*Her first interview with the mayor went too long, because she was still **green** and didn't know which questions to ask.*

foregone conclusion
noun

· ·

odds and ends
noun

noun

an obvious outcome; a result which can be predicted in advance

*Because of the home team's superior defense, it was a **foregone conclusion** that they would win.*

· ·

noun

an assortment of random things

*His desk was covered with **odds and ends**, and it was impossible to find anything.*

level playing field
noun

. . . .

mixed emotions
noun

noun
fairness; equality
*Public schools are intended to create a **level playing field** in education.*

. . . .

noun
positive and negative feelings felt at the same time
*She has **mixed emotions** about moving away; she's excited about the new house, but worried about going to a new school.*

the powers that be
noun

. . . .

the light at the end of the tunnel
noun

noun
the people who have authority
*No changes can be made without approval from **the powers that be**.*

. . . .

noun
hope that a time of difficulty will end
*He struggled to get out of debt for years, but he finally sees **the light at the end of the tunnel**.*

white elephant
noun

· ·

lame duck
noun

noun

a possession that is useless or unwanted, and difficult to get rid of

*The painting is valuable, but no one wants a picture of a slaughterhouse, so it's really a **white elephant**.*

. . . .

noun

a person who is currently in a position of authority, but whose successor has already been chosen

*When a sitting president loses the election for a second term in November, he becomes a **lame duck** until the new president is inaugurated the following January.*

*Now that our company's CEO is a **lame duck**, people doubt that she will be able to accomplish much before she retires.*

second wind
noun

. . . .

the last minute
noun

noun

a new burst of energy or strength to continue a difficult effort
In the last week before the play opened, the actors got their **second wind** *and rehearsed long hours to ensure that it was a success.*
[originally used to describe the sudden ability to breathe more easily which some people feel after exercising for a long time]

. . . .

noun

the latest possible time
She always leaves her homework until **the last minute***.*
Also as an adjective: **last-minute** *Christmas shopping.*

as a **last resort**
noun

• •

the last straw
noun

noun

the final option remaining when everything else has failed
*Doctors consider surgery for weight loss the **last resort** and only recommend it for people who are not helped by diet, exercise, or medication.*

● ●

noun

the last of a series of problems or annoyances, which causes someone to finally give up
*We have put up with a leaky roof, dripping faucet, and heating problems in this apartment, but the roaches were **the last straw**; we are going to move out tomorrow.*

white lie
noun

· ·

salt of the earth
noun

noun

a lie considered to be harmless, often told out of politeness
*I told her she looked nice, but it was a **white lie**; her dress was really ugly.*

· ·

noun

a person who is decent, honest, kind, and unpretentious
*Her parents are very nice people, **the salt of the earth**.*
Often used as an adjective: ***salt-of-the-earth** people.*

yellow journalism
noun

. . . .

the lesser of two evils
noun

noun
journalism that is sensationalist and biased
*That newspaper will print anything to sell papers – it's all gossip and **yellow journalism**.*
Also *yellow press*.

. . . .

noun
an option which is bad, but still better than the alternative
*I wasn't impressed with either of the candidates, but I voted for **the lesser of two evils**.*

red tape
noun

• •

small talk
noun

noun
excessive regulations and bureaucracy
We had to deal with a lot of **red tape** *to get the proper visa to travel here.*
[From the reddish-colored tape or ribbon that was once used to tie together bundles of legal documents]

• •

noun
polite conversation on unimportant topics; chat
He made **small talk** *with all of the guests at the party.*

the tip of the iceberg
noun

· ·

no time to lose
noun

noun

a small but easily recognized part of a much larger problem or issue

*The corruption scandals reported in the news are only the **tip of the iceberg**.*

[a reference to the fact that the biggest part of an iceberg is hidden underneath the water – only the tip is visible]

· ·

noun

no extra time, meaning it is necessary to do something right away

*There is **no time to lose**, so let's get to work.*

double-edged sword
noun

· ·

sticking point
noun

noun

something that has the potential both to help and to hurt
*His talent is a **double-edged sword**: it brings him success, but has also limited his options.*

. . . .

noun

a controversial issue that is an obstacle to making an agreement
*They are close to signing a contract, but the number of vacation days is still a **sticking point**.*

zero tolerance
noun

• •

mint condition
noun

noun

a policy of punishing even minor offenses

*The school has instituted policy of **zero tolerance** for dress code violations; last week, a student got detention for forgetting to wear a tie.*

Also as an adjective: *a **zero-tolerance** approach to law enforcement.*

．．．．．．．．．．．．．．．．．．．．．．．．．．．．．．．．

noun

in excellent condition, as if new

*These antique toys are very valuable because they are still in **mint condition**.*

Also as an adjective: *a **mint-condition** car.*

[in reference to *mint*, a place where coins are made]

the upper hand
noun

· ·

bad blood
noun

noun

the better position in a situation; the advantage
When the other team's best player was injured, we gained the **upper hand**.

· ·

noun

hostility due to past events; ill will; antagonism; hatred
There has been **bad blood** *between them ever since the lawsuit ten years ago.*

game plan
noun

. . . .

the cutting edge
noun

noun
a strategy
*What is your **game plan** for increasing profits?*

. . . .

noun
the forefront of progress within a field
*This scientist is doing work on **the cutting edge** of physics research.*
Also used as an adjective: ***cutting-edge*** *technology.*

his **Achilles heel**
noun

· ·

a clean slate
noun

noun
the one weak spot of an otherwise strong person
Though I am generally good in English, his first question found
my Achilles heel*: my ignorance of spelling rules.*
[in reference to the character *Achilles* in Greek mythology,
who could only be injured on his heel]

- -

noun
a fresh start, with any previous mistakes forgiven or forgotten
He moved to a new school, where he could start over with **a**
clean slate*.*

gray area
noun

. . . .

face value
noun

noun

an issue about which there is no clear answer, or where conventional standards don't seem to apply

*A lot of Internet businesses operate in a **gray area**, and no one is sure what laws should apply to them.*

[from the idea that some issues are *neither black nor white*]

. . . .

noun

1. the value printed on a ticket, note of currency, etc.; 2. the apparent or superficial meaning of something

*We paid more than **face value** for the concert tickets.*

*If you take his last speech at **face value** it sounds like he is planning radical changes.*

about face
noun

· ·

what it takes
noun

noun

a complete reversal; a U-turn

*After ten years of supporting the same party he did an **about face** and started voting for the opposition.*

• •

noun

the qualities required to accomplish something

*Your daughter has **what it takes** to be a professional musician.*

a **vicious circle**
noun

. . . .

the **eleventh hour**
noun

noun

a cycle of negative effects that build off of one another, resulting in a worsening situation; a downward spiral
*Some overweight children get caught in a **vicious cycle**: they don't excel at athletics, so they get less exercise, which in turn makes them even more overweight.*
Also ***vicious cycle***

. . . .

noun

the last possible moment
*They waited until the **eleventh hour** to make plans for their trip, and had trouble getting a hotel room.*
Also as an adjective: *an **eleventh-hour** effort to conclude the talks.*

bitter pill
noun

• •

uncharted waters
noun

noun

an unpleasant fact that is difficult to accept
*The knee injury that ended his tennis career was a **bitter pill**, but he became a successful coach.*

• •

noun

a new or unfamiliar situation
*Advances in biotechnology are taking scientists into **uncharted waters** requiring new ethical guidelines.*
[*uncharted* means 'unmapped or unexplored']

rule of thumb
noun

. . . .

hard feelings
noun

noun
a general or approximate guideline
*When cooking rice, a good **rule of thumb** is to use two parts water to one part rice.*

· ·

noun
negative feelings of resentment or bitterness
*They are no longer in business together, but they are still friends and there are no **hard feelings** about the end of their partnership.*

true colors
noun

· ·

bells and whistles
noun

noun

a person's real or authentic character

*He seems very calm and polite, but his angry outburst yesterday revealed **his true colors**.*

. . . .

noun

attractive but unnecessary extra features

*For a little bit more money you can get the deluxe version of the car with all the **bells and whistles**.*

salad days
noun

· ·

a labor of love
noun

noun

the days of one's youth, regarded either as a time of inexperi-
ence or as a peak or heyday
*We recalled the rash decisions of our **salad days**.*
*His performance has declined since his **salad days**.*
[from Shakespeare's *Anthony and Cleopatra: my **salad days**,
when I was green in judgment*]

. . . .

noun

a project undertaken purely out of pleasure or interest
He paints portraits for money, but his still-life paintings are a
labor of love.

olive branch
noun

• •

seeing **the big picture**
noun

noun

a gesture of peace

*After a hard-fought campaign, the winning politician offered his opponents an **olive branch** by inviting them to join his cabinet.*

• •

noun

the broad perspective on an issue; the overview

*The proposal should focus on **the big picture**; we don't want to get bogged down in the details.*

ill-gotten gains
noun

· ·

quantum leap
noun

noun

profits or benefits acquired unfairly or illegally
*Robin Hood is both a thief and a hero, because he shares his **ill-gotten gains** with the poor.*

· ·

noun

a sudden and significant improvement or advance
*In the past decade there has been a **quantum leap** in our scientific understanding of human genetics.*
[from Physics, where a *quantum leap* (also ***quantum jump***) is the abrupt shift of an electron within an atom from one energy state to another]

the state of the art
noun

· ·

recipe for disaster
noun

noun

the latest, most up-to-date technology
*Her new stereo is the **state of the art** in audio equipment.*
Also as an adjective: ***state-of-the-art** technology.*

· ·

noun

a plan or set of circumstances that is doomed to produce terrible results
*Assigning the two of them to work on a project together is a **recipe for disaster**.*

hollow victory
noun

• •

Pyrrhic victory
noun

noun

a victory that accomplishes or signifies nothing

*He won the race, but since all of the best competitors had dropped out, it was **a hollow victory**.*

. . . .

noun

a victory that comes at too high a cost, leaving the winner worse off

*Nuclear deterrence is based on the fact that even for the winner a nuclear war would result in a **Pyrrhic victory**.*

[A reference to an incident in ancient history (279 BC), when the army of King *Pyrrhus* of Epirus experienced such huge losses in defeating the Romans that he declared: 'One more such victory and I shall be lost.']

ivory tower
noun

● ●

a change of pace
noun

noun

a place that is insulated from the concerns of the real world
To really understand social issues, he needs to get away from the **ivory tower** *of university life.*

• •

noun

a change from what is usual or ordinary
She usually drinks coffee every morning but today she's having tea for **a change of pace**.

the bottom line
noun

· ·

across the board
adverb

noun

the most important consideration or conclusion; the main point

*We talked about a lot of techniques for time management, but **the bottom line** is that we just need to get more done.*

[from the use of *the bottom line* in accounting, where it refers to the final total of a balance sheet]

• •

adverb

for all; in every category

*The new budget makes cutbacks in government services **across the board**, from highways to education.*

at odds with established theory
adverb

· ·

speaking **off the cuff**
adverb

adverb
in contradiction to; in disagreement or conflicting with
*His account of events is **at odds with** the story published in the newspaper.*

• •

adverb
without any preparation
*Everyone was impressed when he gave a fantastic speech **off the cuff**.*

now and then
adverb

. . . .

hand in hand
adverb

adverb
occasionally
*He doesn't exercise much, but he does go biking **now and then**.*

· ·

adverb
1. while holding hands; 2. in close association; jointly
*Couples walked down the street **hand in hand**.*
*Low unemployment often goes **hand in hand** with inflation.*

He was left **in the dark**
adverb

• •

down the road
adverb

adverb

without important information; uninformed

*She was upset that they had kept her **in the dark** about their plan to sell the house.*

. . . .

adverb

in the future

*This may seem like a risky investment now, but I am confident that it will pay **down the road**.*

prepared **ahead of time**
adverb

· ·

at stake
adverb

adverb
in advance; beforehand
*He practiced an acceptance speech **ahead of time** just in case he won the prize.*

. . . .

adverb
at risk; in question
*The national championship is **at stake** in this game.*

in the wake of
adverb

. . . .

through thick and thin
adverb

adverb
as a consequence of; in the aftermath of
In the wake of *the recent earthquake we decided to redesign the building for stability.*

. . . .

adverb
through good times and bad times; in all circumstances
*Married couples vow to support each other **through thick and thin**.*

no accomplishments **to speak** of
adverb

• •

without a doubt
adverb

adverb
worth mentioning
*He doesn't have any savings **to speak of**; he spends all of his money on entertainment.*

. . . .

adverb
certainly; absolutely; unquestionably
*It was **without a doubt** the worst book I have ever read.*

on top of everything else
adverb

· ·

out of the blue
adverb

adverb

in addition to; besides

On top of all of his other accomplishments, he is now captain of the hockey team.

. . . .

adverb

without any warning; unexpectedly; out of nowhere

I hadn't seen him in months, but he called me out of the blue last week and invited me to dinner.

as far as he **knows**
adverb

• •

on one's mind
adverb

adverb

based on the information (a person) has; to the best of (a person's) knowledge

*She isn't here yet, but **as far as** I **know** she is still planning to come.*

• •

adverb

in one's thoughts; preoccupying one

*I have a lot **on my mind** right now.*

*That incident has been **on his mind** lately.*

behind closed doors
adverb

. . . .

on behalf of someone
adverb

adverb
in secret; out of public view
The government eventually signed the treaty, but we may never know what bargains were made **behind closed doors** *to make it happen.*

· ·

adverb
as a representative of someone; in the interest of someone
He wrote a letter **on behalf of** *his mother, asking the company to give her a refund.*

be that as it may
adverb

· ·

under the table
adverb

adverb
nevertheless
*Some say that printed books are becoming obsolete; **be that as it may**, publishing remains a dynamic and prosperous business.*

. . . .

adverb
without proper permission or disclosure; illegally
*He was getting paid **under the table** to avoid taxes.*
[See *above board*]

we experienced it **at first hand**
adverb

. . . .

on and off
adverb

adverb
personally; directly; in person
*I had heard that the Grand Canyon was impressive, but I didn't appreciate its enormity until I saw it **at first hand**.*

. . . .

adverb
with interruptions; intermittently
*It rained **on and off** all night, but never for very long.*

in a nutshell
adverb

. . . .

down the line
adverb

adverb
in a short summary; very briefly
*This book covers the major points of the topic **in a nutshell**.*

. . . .

adverb
in the future; eventually
*This may seem like a good policy now, but it could cause major problems **down the line**.*

to a fault
adverb

. . . .

by word of mouth
adverb

adverb
excessively; so much that it causes problems
*She is careful **to a fault**; it takes her forever to finish anything.*

. . . .

adverb
through informal conversation
*They didn't have enough money to advertise in the newspaper, but they got a lot of publicity **by word of mouth**.*
Also as an adjective: ***word-of-mouth** advertising.*

behind someone's **back**
adverb

. . . .

behind the scenes
adverb

adverb

when someone is not around

*It is unfair to criticize him **behind his back**, when he can't defend himself.*

*You shouldn't say anything **behind her back** that you wouldn't say to her face.*

. . . .

adverb

out of public view

*The agreement between the two leaders seemed spontaneous, but a lot of negotiations were conducted **behind the scenes** to make it happen.*

[a reference to theaters, where preparations take place behind the scenery, out of sight of the audience]

all of a sudden
adverb

• •

beyond the shadow of a doubt
adverb

adverb

without any warning; instantly

*We were walking in the park when **all of the sudden** the lights went out.*

. . . .

adverb

without any doubt at all; for certain

*We now know **beyond a shadow of a doubt** that the Vikings reached North America centuries before Columbus.*

in the balance
adverb

· ·

in over one's head
adverb

adverb
at stake; at risk
*Applying to college is very stressful; sometimes it feels like your entire future is **in the balance**.*

. . . .

adverb
in a situation for which one is not qualified or prepared
*He got **in over his head** when he agreed to do all of the paperwork for the project.*

by the book
adverb

· ·

as far as someone **is concerned**
adverb

adverb
according to the rules or directions; correctly
*There weren't any violations—she did everything **by the book**.*

. . . .

adverb
in someone's opinion
*I thought it was great, but **as far as** he **was concerned** it was the worst movie of the year.*

in no time
adverb

· ·

by virtue of
adverb

in no time

adverb

very quickly; right away

*The cookies are almost done; they will be ready **in no time**.*

· ·

by virtue of

adverb

because of; on the basis of

*She got the job **by virtue of** her superior language skills.*

for the time being
adverb

· ·

by all means
adverb

adverb
for now; at this time, but not necessarily in the future
*Let's keep this project a secret **for the time being**.*

. . . .

adverb
certainly; definitely
*If you go to that restaurant, **by all means** try the salmon.*
See by no means.

by no means
adverb

• •

You're late, **as usual.**
adverb

adverb
absolutely not; not at all
*She is a talented singer but **by no means** the best in the choir.*
See by all means.

. . . .

adverb
as ordinarily or habitually happens; like always
*I planned to study before class today, but **as usual** I overslept.*

back to square one
adverb

· ·

in view of
adverb

adverb
back to the point where one started, as if no progress had been made
*If this doesn't work, we can go **back to square one**.*
*Their first plan failed, so now they are **back at square one**.*

· ·

adverb
considering; taking into account
*His writing is especially impressive **in view of** the fact that English is not his first language.*

in the long run
adverb

. . . .

by the way
adverb

adverb
after a long time; in the end; eventually
*It may seem hard to save money for retirement now, but **in the long run** you will be very glad that you did.*

• •

adverb
incidentally
*I read that book you lent me. **By the way**, did you know the author lives near here?*

for the most part
adverb

· ·

It has not happened **as yet.**
adverb

adverb
in general; mostly
*Her grades this year were good **for the most part**.*

· ·

adverb
up to the present time; as of now
*They will be hiring a new secretary, but **as yet** they have not done so.*

in light of
adverb

· ·

for good measure
adverb

adverb

considering; because of; taking into account
*She was given a lighter punishment **in light of** the fact that this was the first time she had broken the rules.*

· ·

adverb

in addition; beyond what is needed
*The recipe called for four cloves of garlic, but I added two more **for good measure**.*

against all odds
adverb

· ·

by hand
adverb

adverb
despite it being very unlikely; incredibly, unexpectedly
__Against all odds__, she won her match against the five-time state champion.
He recovered from the operation and, __against the odds__, was able to walk again.

. . . .

adverb
without using a machine
Delicate fabrics like cashmere should be washed __by hand__.

from the looks of
adverb

· ·

on the spot
adverb

adverb

based on the appearance of something; apparently

From the looks of the orientation assembly, there must be fewer students at school this year.

The bake sale is raising a lot of money this year, by the looks of it.

• •

adverb

1. immediately; 2. in an awkward position where one is forced to make a difficult decision right away

She didn't expect to get an answer for several weeks, but the accepted her application on the spot.

He put me on the spot by proposing marriage in front of his whole family.

with one voice
adverb

. . . .

warts and all
adverb

adverb
unanimously; in unison
*The company's employees opposed the policy **with one voice**.*

. . . .

adverb
including a person's faults as well as his or her positive qualities
*Parents love their children unconditionally, **warts and all**.*

as a matter of fact
adverb

· ·

on behalf of
adverb

adverb
actually; in fact
*The outcome of a military conflict is not simply based on casualties; **as a matter of fact**, the Union Army suffered greater losses than the Confederate Army in the American Civil War.*

. . . .

adverb
1. in the interest of; in support of; 2. as a representative of; in the name of
*We are raising money **on behalf of** the local food bank.*
*The lawyer wrote a letter **on behalf of** his client, requesting a meeting.*

as a rule
adverb

· ·

one by one
adverb

adverb
usually; in general
*I don't like documentary films **as a rule**, but this one is extremely interesting.*

. . . .

adverb
individually; in succession; one at a time
*When your work seems overwhelming, it can be helpful to deal with your assignments **one by one**, instead of trying to accomplish everything at once.*

on the loose
adverb

· ·

under the weather
adverb

adverb
out in public
*The community was concerned when they heard that a convict had escaped from prison and was **on the loose**.*

. . . .

adverb
sick; not feeling well
*She's not coming in to work today, because she's feeling a bit **under the weather**.*

In the affirmative
adverb

· ·

In the negative
adverb

adverb
positive answer; yes
*When she asked the committee if they thought funding the project was a good idea, they responded **in the affirmative**.*

· ·

adverb
negative answer; no
*He asked the woman for a date, but she answered **in the negative**.*

on the spur of the moment
adverb

· ·

adverb
spontaneously or impulsively; without prior planning
*They were supposed to stay home this weekend, but **on the spur of the moment** they decided to go camping instead.*

. . . .